THE LITTLE BOOK OF
Healthy Organizations

Published titles include:

The Little Book of Restorative Justice, by Howard Zehr

The Little Book of Conflict Transformation, by John Paul Lederach

The Little Book of Family Group Conferences, New-Zealand Style, by Allan MacRae and Howard Zehr

The Little Book of Strategic Peacebuilding, by Lisa Schirch

The Little Book of Strategic Negotiation, by Jayne Seminare Docherty

The Little Book of Circle Processes, by Kay Pranis

The Little Book of Contemplative Photography, by Howard Zehr

The Little Book of Restorative Discipline for Schools, by Lorraine Stutzman Amstutz and Judy H. Mullet

The Little Book of Trauma Healing, by Carolyn Yoder

The Little Book of Biblical Justice, by Chris Marshall

The Little Book of Restorative Justice for People in Prison, by Barb Toews

El Pequeño Libro De Justicia Restaurativa, by Howard Zehr

The Little Book of Cool Tools for Hot Topics, by Ron Kraybill and Evelyn Wright

The Little Book of Dialogue for Difficult Subjects, by Lisa Schirch and David Campt

The Little Book of Victim Offender Conferencing, by Lorraine Stutzman Amstutz

The Little Book of Healthy Organizations, by David R. Brubaker and Ruth Hoover Zimmerman

The Little Books of Justice & Peacebuilding present, in highly accessible form, key concepts and practices from the fields of restorative justice, conflict transformation, and peacebuilding. Written by leaders in these fields, they are designed for practitioners, students, and anyone interested in justice, peace, and conflict resolution.

The Little Books of Justice & Peacebuilding series is a cooperative effort between the Center for Justice and Peacebuilding of Eastern Mennonite University (Howard Zehr, Series General Editor) and publisher Good Books (Phyllis Pellman Good, Senior Editor).

THE LITTLE BOOK OF
Healthy
Organizations

Tools for Understanding and
Transforming Your Organization

DAVID R. BRUBAKER
RUTH HOOVER ZIMMERMAN

Good Books

Intercourse, PA 17534
800/762-7171
www.GoodBooks.com

Credits

The Organizational Tree diagram and concept on page 8 is courtesy of Joanne Dietzel.

Larry Greiner's Model of Organizational Growth on page 19 is adapted and reprinted by permission from *Harvard Business Review*. Copyright 1972 by the President and Fellows of Harvard College. All rights reserved.

Sections from Chapters 3, 6 and 7 (on leadership, change and conflict) were adapted for use in *Promise and Peril: Understanding and Managing Change and Conflict in Congregations* by David R. Brubaker (Herndon, Virginia: Alban Institute, 2009).

The Iceberg of Culture diagram on page 38 is the authors' application of Edgar Schein's three levels of organizational culture. See Edgar Schein, *Organizational Culture and Leadership* (San Francisco: Jossey-Bass, 2004).

Cover photograph by Howard Zehr

Design by Cliff Snyder

THE LITTLE BOOK OF HEALTHY ORGANIZATIONS
Copyright ©2009 by Good Books, Intercourse, PA 17534
International Standard Book Number: 978-1-56148-664-9
Library of Congress Catalog Card Number: 2009017182

Library of Congress Cataloging-in-Publication Data

Brubaker, David R.
 The little book of healthy organizations : tools for understanding and transforming your organization / David R. Brubaker & Ruth Hoover Zimmerman.
    p. cm.
  ISBN 978-1-56148-664-9 (pbk. : alk. paper) 1. Organizational sociology.
2. Leadership. 3. Corporate culture. 4. Organizational change. I. Zimmerman, Ruth Hoover. II. Title.
  HM786.B78 2009
  302.3'5--dc22   2009017182

Table of Contents

About this Book

We live in a world of organizations, from not-for-profits to for-profits to governmental agencies. But we don't just *belong* to organizations. They shape our very *identities*, from the hospital where we're born to the retirement community where many of us will complete our years.

Because organizations have such an impact upon our lives, it's in our interest to understand them, not simply to comprehend their impact but also to help them become healthier and more fulfilling places to work and grow. We believe that as our organizations become healthier, our families and our societies will, too. This *Little Book* is designed to contribute to that goal.

Organizational leaders are the primary audience of this *Little Book*, including those in for-profit, not-for-profit, or governmental settings. We understand "leadership" to be a group function that is not limited to one individual at the top of the organizational pyramid. For example, most not-for-profit organizations nest the leadership function in their top staff, and the governance function in their board; whereas, religious congregations are led by a combination of ordained clergy and elected laypersons. Both groups—board and staff—we consider to be "leaders" of the organization, despite their differing functions.

Based on our understanding of the research on organizational leadership and on our experience with scores of organizations, we believe that effective leaders strive to follow these three maxims:

1. Know Yourself

2. Know Your Organization

3. Know Your Environment

About this Book

This *Little Book* is designed to increase your awareness of your organization as a system, and to help you begin to map the various environments in which your organization functions. Self-awareness is a journey that goes beyond the scope of this *Little Book*, and is best guided by a counselor, mentor, peer accountability group, or spiritual director.

What does it mean to take a "systems approach" to organizations? We view organizations as organic (living), interconnected, and open. An organization is a living organism, which means that at some point it was born and at some point it will likely cease to exist. An organization also is interconnected—meaning that its various components or departments mutually influence each other. Finally, an organization is an open system—it receives resources and other inputs from its environment but also acts back upon the environment.

A final word regarding the stories contained in this book: You will note that each chapter includes stories from organizations with which we have worked or consulted. Many of our stories come from the Center for Justice and Peacebuilding at Eastern Mennonite University in Harrisonburg, Virginia, where the two of us initially developed a working relationship. We have decided to share stories of both good times and bad, believing that honesty about our organizational experiences is more likely to resonate with readers than happy stories alone.

About the Authors

We draw heavily on our experiences in this book so we want you to know a bit about our backgrounds.

David

I graduated from college in 1980 with a degree in Business Administration, and two years later headed to Brazil with Mennonite Central Committee as assistant program director. I was surprised primarily by how much I didn't know about management and administration, so shortly after returning from three years in Brazil I began an MBA program at Eastern University in Pennsylvania.

The MBA courses and additional administrative experience prepared me well for a five-year contract as executive director of Seeds of Hope, a faith-based community development organization in Arizona. During that time I began to do more workplace mediation and to consult with organizations on change, conflict, and leadership issues. Organizations increasingly fascinated me, so in 1997 I decided to begin a Ph.D. program at the University of Arizona, specializing in the sociology of organizations. In 2004 I joined the Center for Justice and Peacebuilding faculty at Eastern Mennonite University in Harrisonburg, Virginia. This book reflects the systems view of organizations that I developed through study and practice.

Ruth

Leadership and administration have interested me for most of my adult life. It started when I was a church youth leader at a time when young women often weren't encouraged to lead. My first career was as a nurse and team leader. Later, while living overseas, I increasingly was invited to administrative leadership positions. During that time I took a number of master's level courses in leadership through an extension program of Azusa Pacific University in Southern California.

After starting at Eastern Mennonite University in 1994 as a staff person at the Center for Justice and Peacebuilding (CJP), I moved rapidly into administration, completed a master's degree with a focus in organizational leadership, and for five years co-directed CJP. In addition, I started co-teaching the Healthy Organizations course, first with Vernon Jantzi and then with David Brubaker. It was out of this course that David and I conceived this *Little Book*.

I am thankful for the male mentors in my life who recognized my skills and gifts and gave me room to grow and develop at a time when many women felt stymied and cut off from leadership. In 2007, I joined an international peace, development, and relief non-governmental organization and became the first woman to direct their India, Nepal, and Afghanistan programs based in Kolkata, India.

1.
The Organizational Tree

While every organization can trace its founding to a particular individual or group of individuals, over time organizations take on lives of their own. They are born, they grow and mature, and most eventually decline and die. The great majority of organizations now operating in the United States were birthed in the last 50 years, and only rarely will organizations exceed a lifespan of 80 or 100 years.[1] Human organizations are thus much like the life cycle of other organisms that inhabit this world–they are born, they grow and mature, and they eventually die. Organizations are organic and interdependent systems that require external resources (particularly money and people) to survive and exist in specific environments.

Because of their organic and interdependent nature, organizations are best studied as living systems and perhaps are best understood by comparing them to one. The metaphor that we will use in this book for an organization is a living tree. All trees possess a root system, a trunk, and a branch and leaf system. All have adapted to their environments, and thus a remarkable variety of species of trees exist around the world–from date palms to chestnut trees.

The Organizational Tree

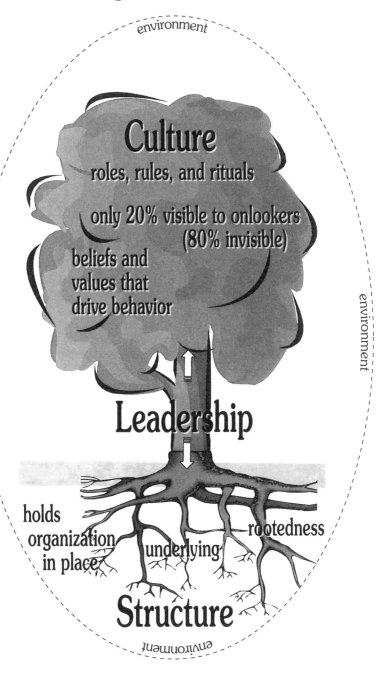

Culture
roles, rules, and rituals

only 20% visible to onlookers
(80% invisible)

beliefs and
values that
drive behavior

Leadership

environment

holds
organization
in place

underlying

rootedness

Structure

The metaphor of a tree helps us to understand the function and inter-relationship of the four major components of an organization—its structure, culture, leadership, and environment.

Structure (Root System)

Every organization possesses a physical structure and a social structure. The physical structure consists of the physical layout of the organization itself—the external buildings and internal office layout of each building. The social structure includes the visible formal structure—usually expressed through an organizational chart—and also a less visible social structure that reflects the informal roles and patterns of interaction that organizational members adopt.

Organizational structure corresponds to the root system because it is the root system that anchors a tree when strong winds howl or seasonal transitions occur. A healthy root system not only provides stability, it also nourishes the tree through access to water and nutrients. Likewise, a healthy and well-designed organizational structure provides both stability and nourishment to the organization. Even if a top leader departs, a well-functioning organizational structure will clarify the process for choosing a successor.

Culture (Leaf and Branch System)

Every organization possesses a unique organizational culture. Shaped by the influence of organizational founders and by subsequent experiences and members, an organization's culture defines the values and behaviors that are considered appropriate if not honorable within the organization. New members who enter an organization's culture often are surprised by the expectations and unspoken rules that longer-tenured members simply assume to be normal. The organization's culture thus serves not only to guide behaviors but also to demarcate the boundary between "insiders" and "outsiders."

Organizational culture corresponds with the branch and leaf system primarily because so much is hidden from outsiders. In summer, the visible branches and leaves of a deciduous tree constitute only 10 to 20 percent of the overall branch and leaf system. The remaining 80 to 90 percent can be viewed and understood only by someone willing to climb the tree and experience it from the inside. Organizational culture is also mostly hidden to outsiders. While it is possible to understand an organization's culture, it is never easy to do so. Organizational culture is capable of being understood only by those willing to enter it. We will explore a model for understanding culture in Chapter 4 of this book.

> **Organizational culture is capable of being understood only by those willing to enter it.**

Leadership (The Trunk)

The trunk of a healthy tree connects the root system (structure) and leaf and branch system (culture), allowing the nutrients from the soil to flow upward and nourish the entire tree. A healthy trunk is neither too rigid nor overly flexible, but will bend slightly when strong winds blow so that it does not snap. The growth of a tree is most visible in its trunk, where we can chart the evidence of years of slow but usually steady expansion.

Organizational leadership corresponds with the trunk of a tree. Healthy leaders understand that they are a critical link between the organization's structure and culture, and are content to pass on the nutrients from the root system to the fruit-bearing parts of the tree. They are neither overly rigid nor overly flexible, but can bend with the times without either snapping due to inflexibility or whipping back and forth due to a lack of fortitude. Like the trunk of a tree, when leaders are performing at their best, the evidence of their efforts appears in the new leaves, flowers, and fruit produced—the trunk itself remains rather unremarkable. The leaves, flowers, and fruit represent the goods or services that an organization produces. Leaders enable and support such production but usually are not the direct producers.

The Environment

Every tree is rooted in a particular environment, and over time its species has adapted to the unique opportunities and threats within that environment. The bushy Gamble Oak found in the American Southwest, for example, looks almost nothing like the magnificent White Oak of the eastern United States. Yet both are perfectly adapted to their environments and share a common family heritage. A successful tree species is rooted in a particular environment and adapts over time to changes in that environment.

Likewise, every organization is rooted in a particular environment or set of environments. Most obvious is the geographic environment, although with multiple locations and branch offices the geographic aspect of an organization can become very complex. Every organization exists in a particular social and political environment, and multiple and sometimes-contradictory social/political environments impact multi-national organizations. In addition to the geographic and social/political environments, organizations must cope with rapidly changing economic and technological environments. Finally, every organization is part of a larger organizational field, consisting of multiple organizations that together comprise an industry.

Change and Conflict

Within the organizational system, processes of change and conflict occur with some regularity. A systems view of organizations often enables us to identify the source of the change or conflict, rather than simply contend with the symptoms. When we look at organizations as systems, we tend to see patterns and causes, not just incidents and symptoms. One common source of change in organizational systems is adaptation to a changing environment—particularly to changes in the economic or technological environment. And conflict often, but not always, accompanies change. In a dynamic organization nested in a rapidly changing environment, conflict is likely to become a familiar presence.

Conflict often, but not always, accompanies change.

This systems perspective differs significantly from the standard production view of organizations, which focuses primarily on the resources that go in, the internal transformation that occurs, and the product or service that comes out. The production view of organizations has its place but is well described in many other books and seems intuitive to managers and leaders. The systems view is neither well disseminated nor intuitive to most leaders, and so will be our focus in this *Little Book*.

2.
Structure – The Roots

Since every organization is an interconnected and organic (living) system, it is important to understand the component parts that together make up this system. As discussed in the previous chapter, the organizational tree consists of a root system (its structure) and a branch and leaf system (its culture) connected by the trunk (leadership), all located within a specific set of environments. An organization's structure provides its rootedness, allowing the organization to remain solid even as particular individuals come and go. Structure can be understood and even mapped at two levels–physical and social.

Physical Structure

Physical structure is the easiest to observe as it refers simply to the layout of the buildings, offices, and other physical space that are owned or operated by the organization. In a university setting we find classrooms, sports facilities, dormitories, and common use areas. In a manufacturing business we encounter open areas where production occurs as well as shipping facilities, warehouses, and offices. A religious congregation tends to have one large room dedicated to worship and other rooms for educational and office purposes.

Physical structure matters because the layout of the buildings, offices, and workspace can dramatically impact social interaction patterns. It's no accident that those who work in the same wing of the plant tend to bond socially, or that academic departments are notoriously departmentalized. When physical space encourages some social interactions but discourages others, we can predict with whom people will connect and with whom they will not.

Organizational leaders need to pay attention to the physical layout of their facilities, especially when building new facilities or remodeling existing ones. If administrators occupy a central building in the university while academic departments are scattered at other sites, it will require significant efforts to encourage social bonding among the dispersed faculty as well as social bridging between the administration and the faculty. (Social bonding refers to the capacity of members of the same group to connect with each other, while social bridging is the ability to make a connection between two or more different groups.)

Physical structure therefore not only predicts social interaction patterns, it also tends to influence social conflict. The classic fight over who gets the corner office is not just about prestige and power; it's also about access and location. Human beings instinctively recognize that location matters, but organizational leaders often are remarkably unaware of the importance of physical structure in their systems. If you haven't done so recently, walk around (inside and out) your facility and consider the following questions: How might physical structure alone explain the connections and the tensions in this organization? Are there any changes that we could make to encourage healthy connection and discourage isolation and tension?

• • •

During the 12 years that I lived in Arizona, I worked with a local community college to provide training, consulting, and mediation services. The college consisted of three campuses, with the college administration located at the main campus but instructors and staff scattered across all three locations. Because the college served a very large county, the most distant campus was a two-hour drive from the main campus. This scattered physical structure produced particular challenges to maintaining a healthy system-wide culture, as conflicts and misunderstandings seemed to sprout due in part to physical distance.

After receiving two mediation referrals from the main campus and one from the most distant campus, I talked with the director of human relations regarding the challenges of managing across three dispersed locations. She had noticed the conflict patterns in the system and the need to address issues that were at least exacerbated by physical distance.

The ultimate solution was to establish a system-wide ombuds program, with volunteer ombudspersons (or representatives) recruited from all three campuses to undergo training and provide services. Through annual reports provided by the ombuds program director to the college president, the volunteer ombudspersons and program director were able to chart trends occurring across the system and make recommendations for systemic change. The ombuds program didn't erase the challenges caused by physical distance, but it did provide a mechanism for naming and addressing the problems such distance caused.

— David

• • •

Social Structure

Social structure refers to the patterned ways in which individuals and units within the organization interact. It can be understood at both formal and informal levels. Formally, social structure is portrayed in the organizational chart—generally a hierarchical model that visually displays the inter-relationships among the various leadership roles in the organization. Informally, social structure consists of those unofficial but sometimes even more important informal roles that organizational members adopt or are placed into—organizational historian, plant mediator, or office gossip. It is in the combination of these formal and informal roles that social structure emerges.

Max Weber argued a century ago that formal organizations (what he called "bureaucracies") consisted of a hierarchy of authority (power distribution), a division of labor (role differentiation), and formal rules and procedures (coordination mechanisms).[2] Although Weber was describing primarily government bureaucracies, his conception of what comprises an organization applies equally well to the other two sectors of organizations—for-profit

> **Social structure emerges both from formal and informal roles in an organization.**

and not-for-profit. Over time, organizations tend to structure themselves, both in terms of rules and roles. When we examine the rules and roles (and, in a later chapter, rituals) at both the formal and informal levels, we understand organizational behavior more deeply.

Conflict can arise out of the social structure for several reasons. First, power can be overly centralized in a rigid hierarchy. When those with less power in the system resist the imbalance, conflict results. Second, roles can be so poorly defined that overlapping responsibilities lead to tension and conflict. When two individuals believe they have responsibility for the same area, conflict tends to result. Third, the formal and the informal social structure can be so at odds with each other that conflict emerges from differing perceptions of who really has authority. (We will address this subject in the next chapter.)

One of the most common causes of conflict related to social structure, however, can be explained by an organization's life cycle. As organizations are founded, grow, and mature, they pass through specific life-cycle phases that have been identified in various models by organizational theorists. Most of the organizational life-cycle models are remarkably similar to the human life cycle—beginning with birth and proceeding through youth to maturity, decline, and eventual death.

One of the earliest life-cycle models, developed by Larry Greiner, identifies five stages of growth, each accompanied by a specific crisis in organizational life. The Greiner stages and accompanying crises are as follows:[3]

1. Entrepreneurial Stage (Leadership Crisis)

2. Collectivity Stage (Autonomy Crisis)

3. Delegation Stage (Control Crisis)

4. Formalization Stage (Red-Tape Crisis)

5. Collaboration Stage (Renewal Crisis)

Greiner's Model of Organizational Growth

Stage 1   Stage 2   Stage 3   Stage 4   Stage 5

Size of organization — Small to Large

Age of organization — Young to Mature

1. Crisis of leadership
1. Growth through creativity (Entrepreneurial Stage)
2. Crisis of autonomy
2. Growth through direction (Collectivity Stage)
3. Crisis of control
3. Growth through delegation
4. Crisis of red tape
4. Growth through coordination
5. Crisis of renewal
5. Growth through collaboration

For Greiner, an organization's progression through each stage requires successful resolution of the crisis that accompanies that stage. For example, one or two highly dedicated and often charismatic individuals tend to provide leadership and energy to an organization in the entrepreneurial stage. Over time, however, the growing complexity of the organization overwhelms the ability of the one or two gifted leaders to manage everything. The leadership crisis that results is normally resolved through the introduction of more professional management, and the failure to make this transition is known as Founder's Syndrome.

Likewise, an organization that successfully emerges from the entrepreneurial stage and resolves its first leadership crisis will eventually be faced with an "autonomy crisis" after some time in the collectivity stage. Here, the various departments or units of the growing organization will begin demanding more autonomy from the centralized management structure and push for greater delegation. If these demands for more decentralized decision-making are successfully negotiated (often through the formation of some form of leadership or management team), then the organization proceeds into the delegation stage.

What is significant about the Greiner model is that it ties an evolving formal social structure to the age (or point in the life cycle) of the organization itself. As organizations grow and mature, they can be predicted to adopt ever more formal organizational structures, leading eventually to a "red-tape crisis" that will require genuine "renewal" to transcend. An organization's efforts at restructuring, then, can be a form of proactive conflict transformation. As they grow and mature, organizations can proactively adapt their formal social structures in ways that are consistent with the needs of the organization at that point in its life cycle.

In addition to age, organizational *size* is another critical variable in predicting organizational behavior. For example, formalization tends to accompany growth in size as well as advancing years. An organization of 10,000 employees that is only 10 years old could be as bureaucratic as an organization of 50 members that is 100 years old. The combination of both large size and advancing years (e.g., the Roman Catholic Church) is highly predictive of significant formalization (bureaucratization).[4]

• • •

The Center for Justice and Peacebuilding (CJP) went from being a new academic program at Eastern Mennonite University (EMU) in 1994, with two part-time faculty and one full-time administrator, to the largest academic department at EMU today. CJP is now a complex organization with nearly two dozen full-time employees and an additional dozen part-time employees for its many programs. It is recognized both internationally and nationally as a leading faith-based academic and practice organization providing many services and products to the field of peacebuilding. CJP now includes the Master of Arts degree program along with the Summer Peacebuilding Institute (both started in 1994). The Practice Institute, established formally in 2001, functions similar to an NGO in providing practice opportunities around the world with its trainings and consultancy, and is home to the well-known STAR (Strategies for Trauma Awareness and Recovery) program.

This rapid growth and diversification brought with it tremendous challenges to CJP's organizational structure. The formative years had all the characteristics of Stage 1 in Greiner's model—a visionary, energized founder/leader with dedicated and overcommitted staff. Decision-making was informal with few levels of administration. Few formal policies, rules, or regulations existed. We developed policy as the need dictated or as it was required by the academic nature of the program. Communication was informal, and ready access to the director was available to all in the small department. Innovation and entrepreneurship were key components.

The first rumbles that this structure was inadequate came during years three to five. The director was feeling overwhelmed with all the demands. The department had grown to around eight employees with 30 students on campus, and the Summer Peacebuilding Institute was experiencing rapid growth. More staffing was needed and additional faculty were hired to do practice work in the United States or internationally, and to establish a viable graduate degree program and summer training institute. There were more visions and dreams than arms and legs to carry out the work. The first restructuring included designating three associate directors to carry more of the administrative weight — one for the Summer Peacebuilding Institute, one for the M.A. program, and one for the overall administration.

CJP initially benefited from Founding Director John Paul Lederach's visionary leadership but low need for control. He valued and depended on the associate directors to administer the program's growing needs. The program did not suffer the traditional life cycle stage of the founding director clinging to authority and control and then damaging the organization by an inability to delegate. When that happens the organization becomes entangled in internal conflicts, and the continued growth and health of an organization gets ignored. CJP sidestepped the classic Founder's Syndrome.

However, the rapid development and its demands did burn out or overwhelm the founding director. In the next stage of development, the director became increasingly dissatisfied with his role as lead administrator and the increasing demands of a growing and expanding organization. Collaboration, coordination, and cooperation were all attributes now required to lead the organization. The founding director stepped out of administrative leadership and back into a teaching and practice role, and a new director and associate director were appointed.

Each of the CJP transitions in the Greiner model was marked by a certain amount of dissatisfaction and conflict in the organization. In response to these stressors, external facilitators were consulted to help determine how best to move ahead. As each sector of the department grew and developed its own internal organization, more autonomy and decision-making latitude needed to be negotiated. Leadership made an effort to find and provide both work and social occasions to enhance the social cohesion of the whole, including through committees and task forces that helped to bond the work and vision of the whole.

— Ruth

• • •

Managing Structure

Since organizational structure can be a significant source of organizational conflict, organizational leaders need to understand and manage this critical variable. With regard to structure, organizational leaders could do the following:

1. Pay attention to the *physical structure* of your organization. Observe where the physical structure encourages connections among organizational members and where it diminishes them. Find ways to make connections across units or departments where physical interaction does not naturally occur.

2. Assess where your organization currently lies on the *organizational life-cycle* model, and if your current structure truly fits the needs of the organization. Be prepared to initiate a structure review process if it appears the structure has not kept up with the evolving organization.

3. Notice *conflict patterns* in your organizational system. What appear at face value as personality conflicts or power struggles may be due to systemic fault lines in your organization, such as unclear job descriptions and overlapping lines of authority.

An organization's structure provides its rootedness, allowing the organizational tree to persist and prosper even as individual leaders come and go. It's worth taking the time to nurture the roots, as a failure to do so can produce a potentially catastrophic weakness.

3.
Leadership and Authority – The Trunk

Organizational leadership corresponds to the trunk of a tree. When a tree is healthy, its trunk provides critical nutrients to the leaf and fruit-bearing part of the tree. A healthy trunk is sufficiently flexible to allow some give when strong winds blow, yet sufficiently strong to keep from flapping in the wind. Observers tend to remark on the overall appearance of a tree, usually noticing the trunk only when up close. A healthy trunk is often taken for granted. We notice the rotten ones, however.

Organizational leadership matters. Successful organizations often revere a current or past leader who was particularly effective at organization-building. Founding leaders may take on mythic qualities–such as Henry Ford or Bob Pierce, who founded World Vision. And organizations in difficulty or decline often resort to removing the boss in hopes of improving performance. Whether discussing the CEO of a worldwide corporation or the senior pastor of a local congregation, most organizational members would agree that leadership is very important.

But leadership may matter less than we tend to assume. Organizations are complex systems lodged in dynamic environments. No leader–no matter how skilled–is capable of controlling all the variables involved in organizational functioning. Organizational dynamics tend to be fairly stable over time, and the arrival or departure of a given leader generally does not dramatically change an organization's performance. There is some evidence that leaders matter most as *symbols*. They set a tone for the organization and come to personify its successes and failures. Leadership is indeed very important, but it is not all-important.

As noted in the previous chapter, leaders exist at both the formal and informal levels in an organizational system. Leaders who appear in the organizational chart are presumed to have authority—what Weber called "legitimized power."[5] They are the ones to whom the organization has granted "positional power," the right to make certain kinds of decisions according to their job descriptions. Others may not always respect their authority in the system, and other sources of power may trump their positional power. Nonetheless, such positions taken together comprise the formal leadership structure.

Informal leaders also abound in any organization. The sources of their power may include personal attributes such as intelligence or wit, or may derive from access to other powerful individuals or from longevity in the organization. Informal leaders may not possess formal authority (legitimized or positional power), but their power to influence outcomes in the organization cannot be denied or overlooked. Given the multiple sources of power in any organization, it is common to find some individuals who possess both formal positional power and informal personal power.

Healthy organizations tend to talk openly about power and seek to distribute it widely. This does not imply a "flat organizational chart," meaning that no one position is above any other. Rather, it suggests that organizational leaders tend to view power as an infinite resource (as opposed to "zero-sum thinking" about power) and to encourage broadly distributed decision-making authority. When organizational members believe that they are capable of making their own decisions about a wide range of issues (within normal boundaries such as budget limitations), power struggles tend to diminish.

> **Healthy organizations tend to talk openly about power and seek to distribute it widely.**

Of course, with power comes responsibility. Said another way, with authority comes accountability. Healthy organizations not only clearly delineate lines of authority, they also provide mechanisms—such as open-door policies and complaint procedures—to insure that all organizational members have the right to register a complaint and have it fairly heard and addressed. The unaccountable exercise of power inevitably leads to abuse, whether it's in the White House or the parish house. Healthy systems design ways of monitoring the use of power and addressing its misuse earlier rather than later.

• • •

Almost everyone has access to one or more sources of power. These include expertise and knowledge, longevity and historical experience, intimate awareness of systems and how they work, personal persuasion abilities, and the will and ability to gather others to a cause. There are also a number of informal power mechanisms to draw from in any organization to help encourage leadership to use participatory and consultative decision-making for the health of the organization.

Some years ago there was an uproar at EMU when lead administrators and the board of trustees made certain decisions around a hot-button issue. Many employees felt the decision was very top-down. Anxiety seemed at an all-time high, with some persons feeling they would lose their jobs if they spoke out too strongly. A few of us at CJP proposed and then helped design a representative group of employees from across departments and levels to gather and address these grievances and to look for compelling and pro-active methods to prevent top-down decision-making in the future.

In short, the group had no positional power, but it had other power sources to encourage and push the lead administration to make changes. The outcomes of this process included the creation of a faculty senate and the development of an employee incident policy. The administration committed to a more dialogical effort around hot-button issues, which helped to reduce anxiety among employees. From a leadership perspective, this moved a large, cumbersome organization with a history of an authoritative leadership style to a more participatory method of decision-making with improved employee morale.

— Ruth

• • •

Effective Leadership

What makes for effective organizational leaders? Countless books on leadership have attempted to answer this question, many written as virtual autobiographies by particular leaders who experienced significant career success. But copying another successful leader's unique style seldom produces copycat success. Rather, research on leaders across organizations may point to more universal characteristics than particular biographies.

Level 5 Executive

5 Builds enduring greatness through a paradoxical blend of personal humility and professional will.

Effective Leader

4 Catalyzes commitment to and vigorous pursuit of a clear and compelling vision, stimulating higher performance standards.

Competent Manager

3 Organizes people and resources toward the effective and efficient pursuit of predetermined objectives.

Contributing Team Member

2 Contributes individual capabilities to the achievement of group objectives and works effectively with others in a group setting.

Highly Capable Individual

1 Makes productive contributions through talent, knowledge, skills, and good work habits.

Level 5 Hierarchy

From *Good to Great* by Jim Collins (copyright ©2001).

In *Good to Great*, Jim Collins and his colleagues selected 11 unusually successful U.S. corporations from among an initial pool of over a thousand companies and attempted to identify the factors that led to their remarkable success.[6] Among the organizational factors they identified was a particular leadership style common to all 11 leaders who led the companies during their transition from "good to great." Collins dubbed these leaders "Level 5 leaders," as all were characterized by a striking combination of a very strong will on behalf of the organization and a quiet personal humility.

According to Collins and his research team, the Level 5 leaders did not seek their own success or visibility; rather, they were unwavering in their pursuit of what was best for their organizations. They often possessed a crystal-clear vision of where the company should be headed, but they combined that vision with humility about their own role in leading the organization. In interviews with these leaders, the researchers often were struck by how these demonstrably successful leaders would change the subject if it became too much about them. In contrast with the charismatic, larger-than-life leader often brought in from the outside to transform an organization, these leaders were generally homegrown—having spent years working quietly and competently within the organization.

In our combined 55 years of experience working within organizations and as organizational consultants, we have noted five traits of successful leaders. All have to do with awareness or skills, and thus all can be developed or improved by existing leaders. These traits could be framed as recommendations, as follows:

1. Become self-aware.

Without exception, the most destructive leaders we've encountered have been remarkably unaware of their impact on others. At the extreme are leaders who commit sexual misconduct with less powerful members of the organization–convinced that it's a "mutual" and empowering relationship. Healthy leaders, by contrast, are consistently aware of others and of their impact on them, and they monitor their own behavior to insure healthy interaction.

2. Invite disagreement.

Successful leaders demonstrate in a variety of ways that they value input and feedback, and create mechanisms to encourage such input. Whether through an open-door policy or through skillful listening, healthy leaders demonstrate that they care deeply about the views of organizational members. Leaders who communicate a "you're either for me or against me" mentality inevitably find that they cut out critical feedback–the kind most needed to avoid disastrous decision-making.

3. Self-define.

Successful organizational leaders are not only good listeners, they also are clear with others in the organization about their own preferences, values, and dreams. The dean of congregational consultants, Speed Leas of the Alban Institute, found through his numerous cases that pastors became the focus of conflict for two reasons–either they were authoritarian and people felt dominated and ignored, or they refused to self-define and people became frustrated and angry not knowing what the leaders really believed.[7] Healthy leaders communicate their own preferences, but they also invite other organizational members to share theirs.

4. Think systems.

Successful organizational leaders tend to think of their organizations as integrated systems and not as isolated parts. Even leaders who head a particular department or division are likely to be more effective if they can visualize and verbalize their own piece of the organizational puzzle in relationship to the other pieces. Granted, this systems view of the organization becomes easier to adopt the higher one rises in an organization. But top organizational leaders can encourage others in the system to grow in their ability to be systems thinkers through workshops, system-wide meetings, and mentoring programs that cross departmental boundaries.

5. Know your environment.

In addition to a deep awareness of themselves and their organizational systems, successful organizational leaders also carefully monitor the changing environments in which their organization operates. The successful college president is keenly aware of young people and their changing needs and preferences. The successful business owner listens to her customers and adjusts her company's product line accordingly. The successful not-for-profit leader monitors both the changing needs of the clients his organization serves as well as the fickle funding environment that makes it possible to continue serving them.

• • •

Sanders Achen is the president of Achen-Gardner, Inc., a successful family of companies that includes engineering, contracting, and home construction businesses. The engineering division is the fifth largest engineering company in the entire Southwest, often securing major road construction contracts. Sanders began the business in the 1980s with a colleague named Doug Gardner, who serves as the company chairman. I came to know Sanders in the 1990s through working on community development projects in his hometown of Casa Grande, Arizona.

Those who know Sanders often comment on how self-effacing he is, taking little credit for himself but often praising his employees and colleagues. Because of a well-deserved reputation for treating employees with respect and care, the people who work for Achen-Gardner tend to be both loyal and grateful. In addition, Achen-Gardner as a company, and Sanders personally, invest significantly in the communities where they are based. They partnered with the city of Casa Grande and a local not-for-profit developer to build a community of homes using the self-help model that greatly improved a distressed and neglected neighborhood.

One of Sander's dictums is that "you hire good people and then you support them in doing their job." Rather than hiring divisional managers to administer the various divisions, Achen-Gardner has instead chosen to establish separate but related companies and coached their managers to become true leaders. Despite the ups and downs of the construction industry in Arizona, Achen-Gardner has been consistently successful with this strategy.

Sanders is keenly aware of the changing environments in which the company operates. It probably helps that he is also a helicopter pilot, and thus can take a bird's-eye view to survey the changes throughout the communities where the company operates. Regardless, his instincts are to consider the changing social, economic, and (more recently) climatic environments, and to adjust the company's strategies accordingly. I have never met a corporate leader who is more self-aware, respectful of others, and sensitive to the multiple environments in which his organization operates than Sanders Achen.

— David

• • •

Leadership may be more art than science, but successful organizational leaders tend to be aware of and closely monitor their own behavior and that of their organizations. They also communicate clearly with organizational members and invite disagreement from any who might see things differently. Finally, they constantly scan the various environments that surround their organizations and make proactive changes consistent with the organization's mission, vision, and values.

4.
Culture – Branches and Leaves

The trunk of a tree sustains a complex branch and leaf system. This is where the visible production occurs, as leaves and fruit mature and branches extend their reach. But for deciduous trees in their season, more is hidden than revealed within the leaves and branches. About the only way to observe the 80 to 90 percent that is invisible from the ground is to ascend the trunk into the branch and leaf system. This complex and hidden system corresponds to the culture of an organization.

Whenever groups of people assemble on a regular basis, a culture develops. Culture is normally thought of as something produced by a nation or an ethnic group, but it can also be the property of a family, a work team, an organization, a community, or a region of a country. In recent years, unique cultures have developed among those who frequent certain electronic websites—demonstrating that geographic proximity and face-to-face contact is not a prerequisite for shared culture. Regardless, culture is the property of a group.

Culture is also the glue that holds a group together. It does so by generating shared expectations and by creating boundaries between those inside and those outside the group. Individuals who choose to join the group are generally assimilated into the group's norms and values and often learn a new language. Culture also provides both the meaning and the methods for perpetuating meaning systems. The members of a local religious congregation, for example, share not only a particular belief system but also rituals designed to remind participants of core beliefs and practices. Culture, thus, serves not only to provide shared meaning but also a sense of belonging.[8]

But religious congregations are not the only organizational forms that have a culture. Sociologically, all organizations possess an organizational culture—often initially shaped by the key founder(s) of the organization. According to organizational culture guru Edgar Schein, culture develops when the attitudes and behaviors of organizational founders are viewed as "successful" in overcoming organizational challenges.[9] Once these attitudes and behaviors are institutionalized in the organization's culture, they become the taken-for-granted core assumptions that lie at the bedrock of culture.

Determinants of Culture

In addition to the personality and leadership style of an organization's founder(s), several other internal and external variables combine to determine an organization's culture. These include:

1. **The *geographic location* of the organization.**
   For example, organizations that emerge in the southeastern United States tend to have different organizational cultures than organizations that develop in the Northeast.

2. **The *era* in which the organization developed.**
   Organizations that were founded in the early part of the 20th century, for instance, often behave differently than organizations founded after World War II.

3. **The *size* of the organization itself.**
   Large organizations behave differently than smaller ones, and "bureaucratic culture," for example, is much more likely in large corporations and government agencies than in small, family-run businesses.

4. **The historic *experiences* of the organization.**
   Whether 10 or 100 years old, every organization has experienced high and low points during its existence. Whether described as an "economic crisis" or the "glory years," an organization's historic experiences combine to shape and reshape its culture.

5. **The composition of the organization's *membership*.**
   Although an organization's members are shaped by its culture, they also collectively shape it. Identity markers such as gender, class, country of origin, ethnicity, age, religion, and education level all interact to determine not only individual identity but also group culture.

Importance of Culture

Perhaps because culture is shaped by many forces and is often tacit and taken for granted, its power and presence in organizational life is seldom fully acknowledged.

But an organization's culture can be described, understood, and even mapped. Schein identifies three levels of culture that allow a careful observer to map an organization's culture.[10] These range from the visible artifacts and rituals, to the less visible norms and values, and

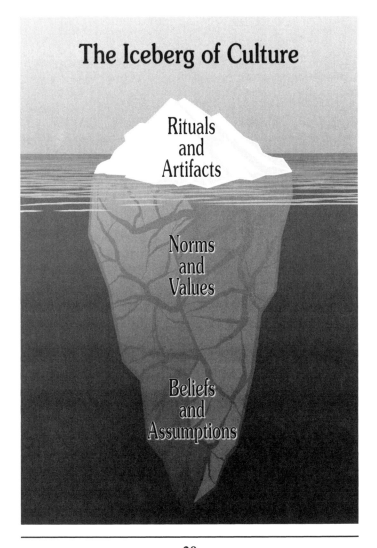

The Iceberg of Culture

Rituals
and
Artifacts

Norms
and
Values

Beliefs
and
Assumptions

finally the tacit assumptions and beliefs. What do the visible artifacts (physical objects) and rituals (processes and practices) in an organization's daily life reveal about its underlying norms and values? And once those norms and values are identified, what might they suggest about the underlying beliefs and assumptions that seem to drive organizational behavior? The Iceberg Model of Culture helps us understand how the deeper levels of culture (beliefs and assumptions), well below the water line, support the visible level of culture (artifacts and rituals) above the water.

The recent emphasis within organizations on developing and even posting "core values" is an effort to make the implicit explicit. Rather than attempting to deduce what the norms and values might be based on observable artifacts and rituals, we can actually compare the espoused values and norms with observed behavior and see if they are congruent. When espoused values and actual practices are not congruent, it is likely that the stated values are not consistent with the deeper beliefs and assumptions in the bedrock of the organization's culture.

• • •

CJP was developed by a relatively homogenous group of EMU faculty and external advisors. In the last century, Mennonites served around the world in relief and development, restorative justice, and related efforts. John Paul Lederach and Vernon Jantzi, along with others, had a strong commitment to lay a positive foundation for this new program at EMU. These global concerns arose from a theologically based commitment to Jesus' mandate for creating peace with justice for all. Additional core values stemmed from the founders' experiences in relief and development work with Mennonite Central Committee (MCC). A critical value drawn from MCC experience is the importance of relationships.

These factors influenced the direction and development of CJP as seen today. The core values and the mission of preparing reflective practitioners of peacebuilding are the central guiding principles. Employees who have joined since then support these values and are dedicated to sowing seeds of peace worldwide.

These commonalities serve to bond the employees together and help create a strong cohesive culture. Visitors and students comment quite often on the hospitality and caring community that they find at CJP. Relationships are important and great care is given to enhancing them. Newcomers usually mention as symbols of this care the potlucks (a meal that all faculty, staff, students, and families are invited to attend), open office doors including the director's, and even the humble but popular candy dish in the main reception area.

We know that many of the students and participants who attend CJP and its programs often come from places where they have seen or endured intense violence. A place of respite is needed as all come together to study and learn from each other. The possible danger in having a strong cohesive culture is that the organization will become risk-averse and thus stagnate or rest on its success. Leaders need the ability to guide the organization between these two polarities.

—Ruth

• • •

Culture generally serves to bond together the members of an organization and provide them with a common frame of reference. But organizational culture is not always a positive force, nor even a benign one. An organization's culture can become a malignant presence when it hinders the organization from pursuing its mission, or when competing subcultures emerge within the organization that detract from a shared purpose. Military organizations have discovered

> **Organizational culture is not always a positive force, nor even a benign one.**

that a macho culture is not an asset when integrating women into their ranks. And universities are known to be bastions of strong subcultures (known as "departments") that often develop unique but seldom collaborative identities.

Organizational culture functions at both an unconscious level and a conscious level. Newcomers to an organization can find it quite difficult to traverse the potential minefields. Longer-term employees already assimilated into the culture may not even understand the questions and confusion that a newcomer may feel in trying to fit in.

When an organization's culture or subcultures become a liability rather than an asset, organizational leaders may attempt to "change the culture" of their organization. Leaders report that such efforts are daunting, difficult, and lengthy. Because cultures are the property of a group, the entire group may bond together to resist the changes that the leaders are attempting. And as with any significant organizational transformation, performance will likely deteriorate before it improves as the organization transitions through the "neutral zone."[11] But research on cultural change, and our consulting and leadership experience, have demonstrated several factors that contribute to successful cultural change. These include the following:

1. **Learn the culture.**

   We're aware of several cases where leaders attempted to change a culture that they neither understood nor respected. It normally takes several years to really understand an organization's culture, and efforts to change it during one's first year are doomed to fail.

2. **Name the strengths and weaknesses of the culture.**

   Several 12-step programs use the motto, "We can't change what we won't name." This is equally true when it comes to organizational culture. By making the tacit visible, an organizational leader who has learned the culture can bring to light aspects of it that are no longer productive for the organization. This may best be done through dialogue and inquiry rather than always directly naming the cultural challenges.

3. **Build a coalition of organizational members committed to cultural change.**

   No one individual can change a culture. Even leaders as gifted and charismatic as Martin Luther King and Mahatma Gandhi knew they needed an entire movement to change a national culture.

Savvy organizational leaders who desire cultural change will ally with others in the organization who share the same goals.

4. Work at cultural change incrementally rather than instantaneously.

No matter how necessary the change may be, efforts to radically and precipitously change a culture almost always fail.

5. Become the change you wish to see.

The essence of cultural change requires leaders to model the desired changes in their own behaviors. Put simply, organizational culture changes when leaders change, because leaders set the tone in any organization. This maxim applies both to the designated formal leaders and also to the informal leaders that exist in any organizational system.[12]

Organizations need a culture that connects members (what Schein calls "internal integration") and also helps the organization adapt to changes in its environment ("external adaptation").[13] An organization's culture generally serves to bind its members together and provide shared meaning and identity, but it can become exclusive and dysfunctional. When that happens, organizational leaders need to initiate a cultural change process that builds upon the healthy contributions of the organization's culture but confronts the negative aspects. When such change efforts are undertaken by a coalition with an understanding of change processes, they are likely to succeed.

• • •

A colleague and I were invited to consult with an ashram that had been established 40 years earlier by a spiritually enlightened founder. After the founder passed away, the community of dedicated followers that grew up around his teachings were deeply impacted by this loss and were catapulted into a period of re-examination and clarification of their identity in light of this change. Although the departed leader had appointed two successors, one was removed from office and the other was greatly challenged by the demands and expectations that had previously been placed upon the founder.

The culture of the organization that had emerged around the teaching of the gifted founder stressed individual spiritual growth in the context of community. However, it also had been deeply conditioned by nearly 40 years of authoritative decision-making by the leader himself. It was very difficult for the community to transition from a single gifted leader making the important decisions for the community to a group of leaders making decisions with the community.

In order for cultural transformation to occur, the community had to name its dilemma and commit to a process of change. This was accomplished through two task force processes involving a diverse group of community members, both appointed early on in the consultation. The first group developed a strategic plan that clarified the identity and mission of the ashram, but also named the challenge of addressing certain theological issues around which the community was polarized. The second group proposed a structure that shifted decision-making from a management board headed by a single individual, to a shared leadership model involving a genuine governance board with an executive director alongside a spiritual board with a spiritual life director.

Through the 18-month process required for these two task forces to complete their work, several community meetings were held to gather ideas, discuss proposals, and reach agreements. Guidelines for dialogue were developed that reflected the espoused norms and values of the community to promote healthy interaction. Over time, it became clear that the ashram's culture was slowly beginning to change. As task force members worked on strategic planning and structure review, they also had to engage each other and the broader community on difficult issues of beliefs and practices.

After about a year involving many ups and downs in the change process, one of the key members involved sent my co-consultant and me an e-mail that included the following paragraph:

"It is so evident how much we have learned this past year. We are approaching problems, interacting, and processing differently. Somehow, just below the level of the group conscious awareness, a subtle shift seems to be happening in our interpersonal and organizational dynamic. I think we are beginning to build trust in a new way. In the grand perfection of things, I think our process has taken so long to allow the time for all this to occur. Without such a shift, whatever we put on paper in the form of a strategic plan or a new structure would not have yielded the desired effect."

— David

• • •

This paragraph succinctly describes the nature of organizational culture and cultural change—it is "just below the level of group conscious awareness" and it is dependent on changes in leaders themselves. Outside consultants can provide the "space" in which cultural transformation might occur, but they are powerless to bring it about.

Organizations change when leaders change. Ideally, those changes occur as individual leaders commit to healthier attitudes and behaviors and model such changes. Sometimes, however, a leadership transition is required to bring about desired changes. Leaders who know themselves and take the time to understand the organizations they have become part of are much more likely to be successful agents of change than are those who lack both self and organizational awareness.

5.
Environment – The Setting

Every organization, like every tree, exists in a particular environment or set of environments. Tree species emerge in a particular environment, and over time successful trees adapt to their changing environments. If a tree is well adapted to its environment it is likely to thrive, but if it's maladapted it will eventually be selected out.

Successful organizational leaders tend to carefully monitor the changing environments in which their organization operates. Failure to adapt to environmental change may have the same consequence for an organization as it does for a biological organism: the organization is "selected out" and disappears. At the same time, an organization that changes to accommodate every passing fad soon finds itself without either core values or customers.

Types of Environments

What are the various environments in which an organization exists? It is often helpful for organizational members to consciously "map" them. Organizations with a multi-national or global presence will operate in multiple environments, and the competing pressures from these diverse environments explain much of the cultural differences and conflicts that emerge in these organizations. Four distinct types of environment that surround nearly every organization include:

1. **Geographic environment.**
   At the simplest level, every organization is located in a particular geographic space. Nearly every organization is headquartered in a specific city or town and draws many of its customers or clients from a particular state, province, or region. Even virtual organizations claim some physical location where the central computer is based. Organizations with a broad national or even multi-national reach operate in multiple geographic environments.

2. **Sociopolitical environment.**
   Related to but distinct from the geographic environment is an organization's unique sociopolitical environment. Not only does the physical geography vary—for example, from the prairie provinces of Canada to the Maritimes—the social and political geography likewise changes. A university with a strong commitment to peace and justice located in a rural southern community of the United States that prizes gun ownership and conservative politics is likely to experience tension with its sociopolitical environment.

3. **Organizational field.**
   Every organization is also nested in a particular organizational field, and sometimes multiple fields. A small florist shop in a downtown location will likely be a member of the community's Chamber of Commerce in an effort to benefit from an association with other businesses. A university will be accredited by a regional or national accrediting agency that encourages adherence to particular norms. And a not-for-profit international development organization is part of the development field, which possesses particular traditions and theories that drive behavior by member organizations.

4. **Economic and technological environment.**
   Finally, all organizations must operate in a particular economic environment, and many operate in multiple environments. Such environments can be transnational (e.g., the countries of the European Union), national (e.g., Nigeria), or regional (e.g., northeast Brazil). Regardless, over time a changing economic environment will dramatically shape organizational behavior. Not-for-profit organizations worry about an economic downturn that might increase demand for services but decrease donations. Governmental organizations fret about the tax base available to support the services they must provide. For-profit companies are anxious about the marketplace's fickle demand for their products or services and the rising costs of supplies and labor.

The Power of Environment

It's difficult to overstate the pressures that these multiple environments exert on organizations and the power that they have to shape organizational behavior. A religious congregation located in a depopulating rural community is likely to lose members, no matter how creative its programming. Public schools are often the victims of changing sociopolitical environments, as an incoming political administration dumps the policies of the previous government and imposes new requirements. And changing economic realities have made it difficult both for small Mexican farmers to compete with American food exporters, and for large American car manufacturers to compete with Japanese and Korean car importers.

Organizational leaders have some influence over these four key environments but a limited ability to change them. They could relocate the organization from one city to another, or work to elect politicians more favorable to the interests of their organization. But in general, an organization's environment acts on the organization more than vice versa. Consider this example of the multiple ways in which environment shapes an academic department within in a university.

• • •

CJP was founded primarily as an academic program to offer a Master of Arts degree in conflict transformation. At the time the discipline of conflict studies was fairly new. It took a lot of work by a very committed group of people to marshal the plan through the myriad university committees and external interest groups.

But while lodged in a Mennonite university, CJP also was located in a primarily rural environment in the southern United States, a changing sociopolitical environment, a dramatically growing organizational field, and an equally fluid technological environment. Each of these external environments placed pressure on CJP to adapt, and there is evidence of adaptation in response to each.

One of the initiatives of CJP's Practice Institute is called "Coming to the Table." This program brings together descendants of slaves and of slave-owners for the purposes of building relationships and exploring areas of common ground. Although the ultimate goal of the program envisions reconciliation and justice, it is modest about the initial steps required to reach such long-term goals. Such a program would probably not have emerged if CJP had been located in south-central Pennsylvania rather than northwest Virginia. The fact that several employees of EMU can trace their heritage back to slave-holding families reflects the reality of EMU's geographic location in a part of the country that experienced slavery.

The most dramatic shift in CJP's sociopolitical field came with the attacks of September 11, 2001. For its first seven years (from 1994 to 2001), CJP consisted of an academic program with a strong focus on international peacebuilding. By September 2001, a decision had been made to add a practice wing to CJP, with a primary focus on supporting faculty practice in international peacebuilding. September 11 changed the focus, however, as an unanticipated multi-million dollar grant to address domestic victims of trauma led to the development and explosive growth of the STAR (Strategies for Trauma Awareness and Recovery) program.

The "boom" in peace and conflict studies programs that began in the 1990s continued in the new millennium. Since its establishment in 1994, CJP could be considered one of the "grandparent" academic programs in the field. But as other programs proliferated around the country, it became increasingly possible for U.S. and Canadian students to pursue a master's degree in conflict studies without leaving their home country, state, or province. CJP had to adapt to this new reality by pursuing new sources of students (e.g., through the Fulbright Scholar Program) and by stressing its unique niche in the peace and conflict studies environment.

Finally, although home computers were common in 1994, the Internet was only emerging as a major force shaping how individuals communicated, shopped, and even received advanced degrees. This has been the change that CJP has been most reluctant to embrace. The program's commitment to face-to-face relationships has inhibited a rush to adopt online course delivery methods. However, as part of its current strategic plan, CJP is exploring what it would mean to offer "hybrid" programs—where a student takes an initial part of the course together with other students and the professor present, followed by a period of online discussion and submission of papers.

— David

• • •

Adapt To or Resist Change?

An organization has essentially two choices in response to changing environments: it can adapt or it can resist. Either or both may be appropriate strategies, and many organizations possess both internal agents of change and agents of stability. Organizational change, then, is usually precipitated by adaptation to a changing environment. There is generally little reason to change when things are going well. However, when market share is shrinking, new student applications are declining, or grants are drying up, organizations tend to start thinking about change. (Change is the subject of the next chapter.)

The more important point for this chapter is that organizational leaders must be aware of the multiple environments in which their organization exists, and they must monitor how those environments are changing over time. With the notable exceptions of war, natural disaster, and economic or environmental catastrophes, most environmental change occurs slowly rather than suddenly and dramatically. Therefore, mapping environmental change is generally more successful over a five- to 10-year period than over five to 10 months, and is easiest to spot over generations.

Consider, for example, how the needs and interests of college students have changed over the last 30 years. In the 1970s, when we headed to college, we were concerned about an outlet in our dorm room for our electric typewriters—not wireless access across campus. Likewise, getting a college education generally meant relocating oneself to a residential campus, not participating in fully interactive courses from home. Colleges and universities may not approve of these changes, but they ignore them at their eventual peril.

> **Organizational leaders must be aware of the multiple environments in which their organization exists.**

Of all the influences coming from an organization's environment, perhaps the most significant comes from the larger organizational field. DiMaggio and Powell famously proposed three forms of "isomorphism," environmental forces that tend to pressure organizations into looking and behaving more alike over time.[14] These pressures arise from the state ("coercive isomorphism"), from the professional fields of organizational members ("normative isomorphism"), and from the organization's field ("mimetic isomorphism"). The latter mechanism operates almost invisibly, as organizations in a field strive to become like the successful industry leaders— often without articulating or even realizing that they are doing so. In short, organizations tend to become more similar over time because of the pressures from the government, professional associations, and competitive organizations in their industry.

In dynamic industries and emerging fields, the nature and composition of an organization's field change fairly rapidly. Although it is, again, most noticeable over years and decades rather than weeks or months, a "snapshot" of an organizational field from one point in time can be contrasted with a later snapshot, and dramatic changes detected.

• • •

We say that organizations can either adapt or attempt to resist the pressures of their external environments. But sometimes the external environment is so unstable that leaders can only attempt to manage the polarities created when all four environmental pressures are pushing at one time—a veritable "perfect storm."

This was the situation for a well-known international development and relief agency situated in a developing country that was going through intense and challenging changes. The agency had been one of the first international NGOs allowed into the country some 50 years earlier as the country opened up to the outside world. The agency grew rapidly, since the needs were so great and there was significant desire around the world to fund development in this country. At one point this agency was the second largest employer in the country, with nearly 3,000 employees! Its reach was wide, and the development efforts included large infrastructure projects such as hospitals, orphanages, schools, and even a hydroelectric dam. The 1970s and '80s were the heyday of this type of large-scale development managed by foreigners.

Significant change became necessary prompted by converging elements. The government demanded that international NGOs facilitate the strengthening of the national NGO sector by releasing a majority of its employees to work in nationally owned and managed NGOs. The sociopolitical environment itself was in serious turmoil, with new ideas finally getting some recognition. Democracy movements were trying to make headway, but chaos and at times violent conflicts ensued between the competing elements.

The agency's solution was to develop a plan whereby it would assist most of the employees in creating new, small NGOs doing the same kind of work they had done while part of the agency. The resulting furor is an example of how the best-laid plans rooted in good intentions can easily go awry in such a demanding and fluctuating environment. Over a period of about six to eight years, the organization downsized from nearly 3,000 employees to a few more than 200 today. It must be noted that the organization put a lot of effort and resources into helping these start-up NGOs. In some cases, it handed over significant assets to the start-ups. It even set up one NGO whose mandate was to provide services to the start-ups in capacity-building, accounting, fundraising, etc. On paper it sounded like a reasonable and doable change operation in which all would benefit.

However, on an administrative trip I made to this country, I interviewed people from various NGOs that developed out of this and also the CEO of the "parent" agency. The level of anxiety, bitterness, and travail that ensued from this process was significant. The newly formed NGOs often felt like the orphaned or rejected child left to fend on her own. Some stakeholders, such as international expatriates who had served at some point with the agency, were very angry—and especially those who were there at the time of the downsizing. Many felt that various aspects of the change process were unfair. Some long-time international funders pulled out. The CEO and board of directors shouldered much of the blame. As a result, the CEO who tried to manage this crucial environmentally-forced change operation had to depart.

—Ruth

• • •

Every organization exists in a dynamic set of overlapping environments. Healthy organizations monitor those environments and make adaptive changes consistent with their mission and core values. Unhealthy organizations tend to go one of two opposite extremes: either they ignore the changes in their surrounding environments and become increasingly irrelevant to them, or they blithely embrace every passing fad and become increasingly indistinct. Neither path leads to organizational success. Strategic adaptations that are congruent with the original mission and emerging vision of the organization tend to produce a more sustainable path.

6.
Change – Growth and Decay

"Change is not made without inconvenience, even from worse to better," wrote Samuel Johnson, the 18th-century English writer. Thus, organizations, like people, generally will change only when the pain of not changing exceeds the anxiety and stress of changing. After all, organizations develop habits (patterns of thinking and behaving) because they're *efficient*—it takes less time and energy to respond in a familiar way than an unfamiliar one.

Change efforts should therefore not be undertaken on a whim. As many survivors of organizational downsizing efforts can attest, major change is too costly, too anxiety producing, and too destabilizing to undergo unless it's truly necessary. And as with the tree metaphor we have been exploring, evolutionary change is generally much more successful than revolutionary change. Trees can adapt over time, but they can't become an entirely new species.

Managing Change

There are, however, some times when an organization needs to commit to a change process. These include the following situations:

- When the external *environment* changes (see Chapter 5).

- When the basic purpose or *mission* of the organization changes (such as the shift in the YMCA away from providing low-cost shelter to providing high-quality health and fitness services).

- When the way organizational members do their work (*process*) needs to change—a change most often precipitated by changes in the technological environment.

- When the *structure or culture* of the organization has become an obstacle to the organization accomplishing its mission.

In short, there are times when organizational leaders need to take the initiative in leading their organizations through a managed change process. Such a process may be part of a regular strategic planning effort (often undertaken every three to five years), or it may take place separately from a formal planning process. Regardless, the basic components of a successful change process are fairly well established in organizational management literature. A number of "stage models" of planned organizational change exist, such as Kotter and Cohen's eight-stage model, but most are predicated upon the following three assumptions:[15]

1. Organizations won't make major changes unless they perceive an urgent, often life-threatening, need to do so. Even then, some in the organization will resist the change.

2. One person alone does not accomplish organizational change, even when s/he is the top leader. A broad-based coalition is needed to bring about change.

3. Successful change efforts are immersed in communication and participation. Organizational members will need opportunities not only to hear about the proposed changes but also to help shape them.

> "During any transition, performance will inevitably decline before reaching the improved desired state."

Another important development in the literature on organizational change is the awareness that during any significant change process things usually get worse before they get better. According to Schneider and Goldwasser, "During any transition, performance will inevitably decline before reaching the improved desired state.... Managing change is really about managing this transition."[16] A remarkable number of organizational change efforts are aborted in the middle of this transition zone, mainly because organizational leaders succumb to resistance efforts and the demonstrably lowered morale and performance in the midst of major transitions.

• • •

John Paul Lederach, an internationally known author and conflict transformation practitioner, founded CJP (then known as the Conflict Transformation Program) along with several colleagues in 1994. For the first seven years of its existence, the program was small enough to be governed by a fairly flat organizational structure and a consensus model of decision-making. Management staff consisted of a director and a full-time associate director of administration (myself), who cared for administrative details.

When the second director, Vernon Jantzi, resigned in 2001, the program adopted a co-director model of governance. I was promoted to co-director for administration, and a senior faculty member (Howard Zehr) became part-time co-director for program. Howard continued to teach in the restorative justice arena. Since this was an innovative attempt at governance from a collaborative, shared leadership model, the committee that designed the model mandated a leadership review in three years' time.

In the fall of 2004, the co-directors, in consultation with the CJP executive committee, decided that a full structure review of both leadership and decision-making was appropriate. CJP had experienced rapid growth since 2001 with the start of both the Fulbright Conflict Resolution grant and the large Church World Service grants for trauma workshops (STAR) awarded after the September 11, 2001 events (i.e. external environment changes). We were experiencing tensions and conflicts with this rapid growth in personnel, funding, and expansion of the mission. As co-directors we hoped that a solid structure review would help guide the program into the future and resolve the tensions. Thus, the executive committee established a structure review committee to determine if the co-director model was still meeting the needs of the program and if any other structural changes might be recommended.

Volunteers from each unit were invited to serve on the committee at a faculty/staff meeting in April 2005, resulting in five committee members (two faculty members, a staff person with Summer Peacebuilding Institute, a staff person with the Center's Practice Institute, and the lone fundraising member of the staff). This committee met regularly beginning in the spring and fall of 2005 to organize a survey regarding the structure, compile the results, and make recommendations to the executive committee.

The results of the structure survey indicated a range of opinions among the personnel as to their satisfaction with the leadership and overall structure. The majority was satisfied but a significant group was dissatisfied with the present model. It became apparent that power was perceived to be inequitably shared across the three sectors—the academic program, the Summer Peacebuilding Institute, and the Practice Institute. The committee formulated recommendations to address this issue among others.

When the recommendations passed from the committee's hands to the executive committee's, overall tension and conflict heightened in the organization. Members of the structure review committee disagreed among themselves on how to move forward and which of the recommendations all members could support. The truism that things get worse before they get better in any change process certainly held. It soon became clear that CJP, even though it is an internation-ally recognized conflict transformation and peacebuilding program, was not going to be exempt from conflict. Under-lying disagreements and tensions erupted in other avenues of the program and among colleagues that were normally quite friendly. Uncertainty and anxiety were palpable in the hallways.

As co-directors we were immersed in this challenging environment. From the beginning of the review, we had been able to lead in a rather non-anxious manner. We were confident that in the end the results would help build a strong, healthy, and creative organization preparing us for the next decade. This is the a textbook example for when leaders must remain non-anxious and use their best skills to manage these anxieties and keep the process moving forward.

The first week after the structure review committee returned its recommendations proved highly stressful for the entire system. The co-director for program came in one day and sent an e-mail resigning his post as co-director, albeit offering to serve on an interim basis. As one of the co-directors I can acknowledge letting the conflict and anxiety also get to me. On one particular morning after reading a copy of a very harsh e-mail sent from one colleague to another, I left the office in frustration and tears. I then took the opportunity to join my husband in his out-of-town trip. I needed time to find a fresh perspective and energy amid what seemed to me a near organizational meltdown. Hind-sight tells me we were not close to that, but at the time, the growing system-wide anxiety was overwhelming.

My leaving for a few days at that pivotal point only height-ened the anxiety in the system. As one of the longest-serv-ing employees at CJP, I was viewed as an always present, dependable leader. Two colleagues who witnessed these responses concluded with great concern that the organization was falling apart.

Fortunately, the co-director for program decided to confront head-on the issues that had surfaced. He convened three afternoon-long meetings of the executive committee that very week. I returned from my trip with fresh energy and a renewed commitment to working through the issues. A faculty representative on the executive committee stepped up to provide critically needed leadership as the committee processed the report and recommendations. The core recommendations were approved and supported by the co-directors and the rest of the committee. Executive committee members also were willing to find processes to address additional issues important to building a trusting and healthy organizational environment. Sometimes things do get better after we all are at our worst!

—Ruth

• • •

Principles for Managing Change

So how can leaders successfully implement changes—even major ones—that are indeed necessary for the health and future of the organization? Perhaps more imperative, how can leaders equip themselves and other organizational members to deal with the nearly constant changes that are impacting our environments,

Managing uncertainty and anxiety is an essential task for leaders who want to either initiate or manage change.

our organizations, and thus ourselves? In an era of outsourcing and downsizing, organizational members can be forgiven for looking at change a bit skeptically, if not fearfully. When the rate of change is high and the environment is complex, organizational members will experience high levels of uncertainty and anxiety.[17] Managing the uncertainty and anxiety is thus an essential task for leaders who want to either initiate or manage change. This leads to three principles of organizational change.

1. **Managing change starts with managing oneself.**

   Because leaders do indeed set the tone in organizations, the leadership's ability (as a group) to manage their own anxiety will determine, more than any other single factor, the group's ability to manage theirs. Organizational members may not always listen to what leaders *say*, but they are constantly watching what they *do*. If leaders are able to honestly name the uncertainty inherent in managing change while demonstrating openness and flexibility to the changes that are occurring, they will send a signal that pending changes need not be feared or avoided.

2. **Do not try this alone.**

   This principle is articulated in virtually all the change management literature. Stories of single, highly principled leaders taking on an entire system and winning exist only in fictional literature and the movies. The reality is that planned change generally happens best when leaders (informal or formal) form coalitions that cross traditional organizational lines. Whether dubbed a "guiding coalition," a "strategic planning task force," or a "change management committee," a group of five to 10 dedicated volunteers recruited and supported by their colleagues from across the organization to study the situation and make recommendations is more likely than any single leader to achieve lasting change.

Such groups have their drawbacks, including the time required for a committee to shepherd such a process through the organizational system. Anyone who has served time on a strategic planning committee can attest to that! But if top leaders actively participate in or at least bless the group process, if there is skilled process leadership, and if a timeline is developed and adhered to, the likelihood of success is appreciably increased. Change happens when a broad-based coalition, widely viewed as legitimate across the system, takes on a major challenge with a limited timeframe and develops realistic recommendations.

Ah, but we all know of many committee or consultant reports that contain brilliant recommendations but only gather dust on a manager's shelf. Despite the enormous effort invested in the information-gathering and analysis stage, and despite the careful thought that went into the recommendations, nothing changes. This leads to the third and final principle of organizational change.

3. Organizations change when leaders change.
Leadership change may occur when one leader leaves and another arrives, such as when one university president is replaced by another. But change can just as easily occur when organizational leaders change their behaviors, despite continuing in their roles. The key is that organizational leaders need to model the behaviors desired in the broader system. As leaders change their behaviors, the culture of the organization will begin to shift. As Trahant, Burke, and Koonce have argued, "To change an organization's culture, you must first change people's behavior."[18] And the first place that behaviors need to change, at least if the organization desires to see change, is among the leaders.

This takes us again to Gandhi's simple dictum, "Become the change you wish to see." One might argue with this truism if she is thinking only of a single citizen in a large country, but there is no doubt that the saying applies to organizational leaders. Put simply, leaders need to model, in their own behaviors and interactions, the changes they wish to see in their organizations. If leaders want a culture where every organizational member takes responsibility for his or her own behavior, they need to begin modeling what such responsibility-taking behavior looks like. And if they desire a decision-making structure that pushes decision-making to the lowest possible level, they need to both change structures and delegate authority. Organizations change when leaders change.

• • •

A major international NGO planned an appreciative inquiry process[19] *for its employees in order to reevaluate its focus and direction for the coming years. Employees were excited about using this new participatory process. In the past, lower-level employees often felt left out of the serious decision-making regarding the organization's direction or focus. The organizational leaders were hopeful that bringing in outside resource persons to guide this appreciative inquiry process would help stem the criticism that non-management employees were often left out of important processes.*

The organizational leaders invested considerable time and money for this two-day event and encouraged all employees to participate. The employees felt excited and encouraged by the end of the two days, and generated new ideas on a number of fronts. Recommendations were prepared and sent to the organization's decision-makers with anticipation for the new and fresh start they would all make together.

But the key flaw in this process was that the organizational decision-makers had not attended the two-day event. They had hoped that the process would improve employee morale, but they had not anticipated that the process might require change and new thinking on their part.

Top leaders turned down all but a few of the key recommendations. The morale of the participating employees plummeted sharply, with some leaving their jobs as soon as they could find other work. The person who shared this story with me said she wished they had never held the two-day event. She felt it was worse to taste this little bit of real partnership in the organization and then have it stifled than to never have had the opportunity.

— Ruth

• • •

The moral of this story is clear. Participation by itself is not enough, nor is leadership's modeling of the desired behaviors. It is the combination of the two—full leadership engagement with genuine participation—that is most likely to lead to successful change.

7.
Conflict – Weather and Storms

Conflict corresponds not only to the violent weather that a tree can sometimes experience, but also to the internal challenges that even healthy trees face. When faced with internal disease or decay, a healthy tree responds with a variety of mechanisms to protect the organism itself, including shedding a diseased part. Experts who examine trees are taught to examine not only the visible parts of the tree itself, but also to consider its root system and the environment in which it is growing. A healthy tree can normally overcome an internal or external threat, while an unhealthy tree is prone to succumb to it.

Every organization experiences conflict, even though each one does so in unique ways. The sources of conflict may vary from the micro to the macro—from intrapersonal pathologies to personality differences to globalization forces—but over time they are inescapable. Various studies have shown that managers spend up to 25 percent of their time managing conflict. And as experienced managers know, during times of crisis, conflict management duties can become all consuming.

Although we tend to assume all workplace conflicts emerge from personality differences or communication problems, there are often other significant organizational sources. While not diminishing the importance of interpersonal factors, leaders should also consider common conflict sources within the organizational system itself. These include the structure, culture, and environment of the organization—the whole "tree" and its setting.

Sources of Conflict

As noted in Chapter 2 on structure, conflict can arise out of the organizational *structure* from one of several causes. First, conflict results when power is overly centralized and those with less power attempt to shift the power imbalance. Second, roles can be so poorly defined that overlapping and thus contested responsibilities lead to tension and conflict. Third, the formal and the informal social structure can be so divergent that conflict emerges from differing perceptions of who really has authority. Leaders who notice patterns in the interpersonal conflicts in their organization will want to consider these possible structural causes.

An organization's *culture* can be another underlying source of conflict. The most common conflict arises when newer organizational members encounter an entrenched organizational culture that they do not share. The conflicts that result tend to be framed by both groups in terms of "right" and "wrong" behavior, as culture provides the values and norms that help us determine what behavior is appropriate or inappropriate. If a leader brought in from outside the organization is perceived to be acting in ways that are counter to the organization's cultural values, conflict is particularly likely and tends to be acute. (And when an outside leader and an inside culture clash, culture normally wins.)

Finally, the multiple *environments* in which an organization is nested also provide the potential for multiple sources of conflict. This is the reason why "town/gown" conflicts (between universities and their host communities) are so common. Academic cultures that value debate and progressive thinking are likely to be in tension with environments that value harmony and traditional values. Universities owned by religious denominations may be particularly prone to internal conflicts due to conflicting environments. The religious/cultural environment represented by the founding denomination clashes with the institutional environment represented by the broader academic field—including the secular universities where most professors receive their degrees.

Approaches to Conflict

Regardless of the source of conflict, the view of conflict in organizational literature has evolved over time, from avoidance to engagement to embrace. Early theorists viewed conflict as an organizational ill that needed to be averted or quickly resolved. The later "conflict as natural" school viewed conflict not as a sign of organizational dysfunction but rather as an inevitable part of organizational life. More recently, a "conflict as functional" movement has encouraged organizational leaders to embrace conflict as it leads to innovation and enhanced decision-making.[20]

Stirring the conflict pot may be necessary in some situations.

A consensus in the field of organizational studies has emerged around an "optimal" level of conflict in an organization. When there is too little conflict it may need to be encouraged, and when there is too much conflict it may need to be reduced. In the middle of this curve, however, lies an "optimal" level of conflict where most organizations seem to thrive. Stirring the conflict pot may be necessary in some situations, but when the pot starts to boil over, a conflict reduction strategy may be needed.

Escalating Conflict

The dean of congregational conflict consultants, Speed Leas, developed a five-stage "Levels of Conflict" grid that demonstrates how conflict can escalate in an organization, such as a congregation, to destructive levels.[21] Leas' five levels are as follows:

Level 5 **Intractable Situation**–A polarized conflict that has spiraled out of control and may require outside authority to resolve.

Level 4 **Fight/Flight**–A conflict that has polarized a group or organization and may require the intervention of an external consultant.

Level 3 **Contest**–A personalized disagreement that may need mediation.

Level 2 **Disagreement**–A sharper difference of opinions that will need to be negotiated.

Level 1 **Problem to Solve**–Issue-focused differences resolved through dialogue.

Organizational leaders are well advised to attend to conflict at the lower levels, and to offer mediation to members of the organization if a conflict has escalated beyond the first two levels. The danger to the organization from Level 4 or 5 conflicts is so acute that earlier intervention to prevent conflict escalation is the most desirable strategy. Where that is not successful, organizational leaders may need assistance from outside the organization to de-escalate the conflict to a more manageable level.

• • •

Both organizational change and organizational life-cycle literature highlight the challenge of transition times for organizations. A little more than five years into its existence, CJP experienced its first major transition when John Paul Lederach, CJP's influential founding director, resigned and left for another institution. CJP at that time was so aligned with the name of John Paul Lederach that some could not see beyond his tenure. I remember one student telling me that CJP would not be able to survive his departure. We did successfully manage that transition. Shortly thereafter we hired another experienced professor and reformulated the Practice Institute. We underwent a growth spurt from grants for our trauma workshops and the Fulbright Scholar Program, and saw robust growth in student numbers.

Perhaps because of the successful growth in our practice and academic programs, tensions were growing in the organization. Role differentiation became a point of tension. The programmatic growth brought new personnel sometimes with gifts similar to those already within the system. Who got to do what became contentious, as did who received adequate recognition and was included in the planning. Those of us in leadership were aware of the simmering conflict but were rather nonchalant at first. After all, we were conflict transformation specialists and thus would work this out among ourselves, right?

However, the conflict started to boil over and it became apparent that interpersonal mediation for the aggrieved parties alone was not enough. What had first appeared to be interpersonal, personality-driven conflicts became more complex. There were underlying structural issues with what appeared to be unclear responsibility designations. Questions about power and inclusion highlighted the need to find collaborative mechanisms across program sectors.

We first established a "listening committee" composed of two internal staff members, but this was not successful as the level of conflict made it impossible for either to be seen as truly "objective." In addition, the new co-directors met individually with each key player in the conflict, both to listen to concerns and also to give counsel on the conflict patterns that had emerged among these conflict transformation professionals. Neither effort adequately resolved, much less transformed, the conflict. At that point CJP leaders decided we needed an external facilitator to help us work through the conflict. While we certainly had enough conflict specialists on hand, it became apparent that too many parties were involved in the ongoing conflict, and it seemed to be escalating. We found a well-recommended facilitator and planned a two-day effort. She called and interviewed the persons involved and then the whole department gathered one day for a facilitated meeting.

The outcome was not immediately transformative. However, the air was cleared, with key players at least feeling heard. Some participants grew tired of it all and simply wanted the conflict to end so they could get on with their work and lives. Leadership was encouraged to find ways to help rebuild trust among affected personnel and the department as a whole, to review decision-making structures, and to find a healthy way forward for the organization. Ultimately, this conflict contributed to the system's willingness to implement a structure review process a couple of years later.

As this experience shows, even with the best of intentions and expert assistance, not all conflicts are resolved or transformed, at least according to our timeframes. Leaders need the skills and aptitude for ongoing monitoring and management of these internal conflicts.

Conflict is natural in an organization, even in a conflict transformation and peacebuilding organization! But with skillful leadership, it can enable an organization to take major creative strides, even in the midst of seemingly difficult times.

— Ruth

• • •

Interventions

Diagnosing the level of conflict and seeking outside assistance at higher levels constitutes the "intervention" end of the conflict management spectrum. At the "prevention" end lie opportunities for organizational leaders to create a conflict-healthy system where disagreement is welcomed and destructive conflict doesn't take root. A conflict-healthy system includes both individual behaviors and organizational mechanisms to manage conflict. It begins with the recognition that leaders set the tone regarding conflict management in their organizations, along with many other behavioral norms.

Leaders who desire a conflict-healthy organization are encouraged to consider the following steps.

1. **Invite disagreement.**

   This was mentioned in Chapter 3 on leadership but must be restated here. Leaders who clearly voice their own preferences but invite others to respond with agreement or disagreement send a message that respectful disagreement is welcomed in their organizations. No other step is more important than this first one.

2. **Encourage diversity.**

   This could certainly apply to ethnic or gender diversity but is intended more broadly here to apply to a diversity of ideas and approaches. Cross-functional task forces that bring multiple perspectives together to address specific ideas and problems encourage the diversity of thought that is generally healthy for an organization.

3. **Reward creativity.**

   Organizational leaders who are threatened by creative out-of-the-box thinking among organizational members tend to subtly communicate that such approaches are not welcome. Leaders who are comfortable with disagreement and challenge will instead encourage creative problem-solving and reward it when possible. (Numerous studies have found that the most meaningful reward is simple recognition as opposed to financial incentives.)

4. Clarify values.

Encouraging diversity and rewarding creativity in and of themselves are insufficient to create a conflict-healthy organization. Leaders who desire a conflict-healthy organization will simultaneously strengthen the center by developing and modeling core values. When the values and beliefs are clear, creativity and diversity emerge around a shared core of principles that reduce destructive conflict.

5. Create mechanisms.

Conflict-healthy organizations anticipate that conflicts will occur and create mechanisms to manage them. Although there is an emerging body of literature regarding conflict management systems, the main principle is that healthy organizations normalize conflict and provide multiple ways to manage it. (Options range from open-door policies to the use of mediation, arbitration, and ombuds offices.)

As we know from the literature on organizations as well as our own experience, an organization's culture matters more than its structure. Therefore, while organizational leaders may be able to structure in a mediation program or an ombuds office, the greater challenge will likely be changing the conflict culture sufficiently so that organizational members will naturally seek out and use interest-based methods of conflict resolution rather than choosing only avoidance (flight) or forcing (fight).[22]

• • •

A young pastor was called to serve a medium-sized congregation of about 200 members located in a suburban community. She had previously served as an associate pastor under an experienced senior pastor and learned the importance both of "going slow" when making cultural changes and modeling the desired changes. In her new assignment, she encountered an entrenched congregational culture that valued harmony and agreement but had no tolerance for disagreement or dissent. When disagreement did surface, it was expressed through intense bursts of anger that left everyone wary of conflict.

The pastor committed first to learning the culture, and to understanding the rules and roles in the congregation. Because she had studied anthropology in college, the role of "participant observer" came naturally to her. She asked questions, tested observations, and in general demonstrated her interest in learning more about the congregation and its ways of being.

Within several years the pastor had earned the respect of the congregation, and with that respect the right to make changes. She decided to concentrate first on the board that met with her monthly, as well as the two other staff in the congregation. The pastor worked with the staff and the board to develop a "relational covenant" that described how they wanted to work together, and how they would deal with disagreements and conflicts when they arose. More importantly, the pastor modeled the behavior called for in the covenant—inviting others to respectfully disagree with her and demonstrating what such disagreement would look like.

The change in the congregational culture was slow but noticeable. After a challenging meeting in which a major proposal for structural change was debated and all members present spoke during a Circle Process,[23] one long-term member remarked on the changes she had observed. "We never would have a discussion like this five years ago," she said. "Either the people who were opposed would have sat there in angry silence, or they would have erupted with accusations and the leaders would have gotten defensive. This time, you welcomed their concerns and they were expressed appropriately."

Because of the pastor's willingness to learn to know the system, to earn the right to make change, and to work with leadership as a group, she successfully changed the culture of a congregation with dysfunctional conflict habits. Even after she left, the new habits continued as the expression of a changed conflict culture.

— David

• • •

Culture changes when behaviors and assumptions change, and leaders' behaviors and assumptions matter most of all. Therefore, leaders who invite disagreement, encourage diversity, reward creativity, clarify values, and create mechanisms for healthy conflict management impact the culture of their organizations. The culture may at first resist, but leaders' persistence in modeling the desired assumptions and behaviors will over time change the

Culture change is never easy and it is often painful. But it is possible.

conflict culture (the norms and behaviors around conflict in your organization).

Managing conflict starts with managing oneself. Consider the kind of conflict culture that you would like to have in your organization. Next, start behaving as if that culture has already arrived. Culture change is never easy and it is often painful. But it is possible.

8.
Conclusion

A healthy tree is compatible with its environment. It boasts a stable root system and supportive trunk that together nourish and sustain the productive branches, leaves, and fruit. Such trees adapt over time to changes in their environment. They manage the threats and storms in their environment primarily through maintaining their own health. We believe that healthy organizations function much the same way. To survive in difficult environments, healthy organizations monitor not only their environments but also their own internal functioning.

We have pursued three primary goals in this book. First, we wanted to offer a digestible systems view of organizations. Second, we desired to place change and conflict in organizations in the context of a broader systems perspective, and to normalize organizational change and conflict as inevitable (and survivable) processes by honestly sharing our own experiences. Finally, we hoped to share our conviction that one way to pursue more justice, health, and peace in the world is to work for it within our own organizations.

We also want to identify three limitations of this book, incurred primarily by our life experiences and by the reality that we were attempting to write a truly "little" book that would be accessible to actual leaders and managers (practitioners) rather than scholars. These limitations are as follows:

There is a significant amount of scholarly literature that underlies a systems view of organizations, and we make only limited reference to it in this book.

In addition to the general systems view of organizations that is summarized in this book, Family Systems Theory (FST) has made significant contributions to our understanding of organizations as emotional systems. Since FST is not discussed in this book, those interested might want to consult Edwin Friedman's classic book, *Generation to Generation*, which applies FST to congregational life but which is applicable to other types of organizations as well.

Both of us have worked in significant management and leadership positions in organizations, but those organizations are almost all in the not-for-profit sector. Therefore, our experiences and examples are overwhelmingly drawn from that sector. We believe that organizational theory and practice can be generalized across all three organizational sectors (for-profit, not-for-profit, and governmental)—but want to acknowledge the limitations of our own experience.

We live in an organizational world, and for better or worse, organizations dominate our lives. As we said at the beginning, most of us are born in an organizational setting (a hospital), we celebrate significant life events in the context of other (often religious) organizations, and many of us will die while in the care of yet another organization. In between, we will spend most of our working hours in educational and work organizations that will deeply impact our lives. Momentous decisions regarding war, disease, and poverty are made in the halls of still other organizations.

Given the profound impact of organizations on all of our lives, we propose that our organizations merit not only our study but also our best leadership. Organizational scholars have contributed much to our understanding of how organizational systems work, and to the role of change and conflict processes in such systems. But now we must look to organizational leaders to take those understandings and apply them in practical ways to create healthier and more life-giving organizations.

We believe that as our organizations become healthier, more peaceful, and more just places to be and to work, the individuals and families who live and work there will also become healthier and more just and peaceable. And as those individuals and families change, so too will the communities and other organizations of which they are part. And as our communities and organizations operate in more just, peaceable, and live-giving ways, so, too, will our societies. In short, we believe that the best way to change the world may be one organization at a time. We invite you to join us.

Endnotes

1 Two notable exceptions are universities and religious institutions, which seem to defy the averages. The Roman Catholic Church and several Orthodox churches are arguably the oldest continually operating organizations in the world.

2 ([1947] 1964)

3 (1972)

4 Although no organization stays static over time, not every organization will become larger and more complex as it ages. However, regardless of size, organizations tend to become more formalized and bureaucratic over time.

5 ([1947] 1964)

6 (2001)

7 See Marshall Shelley and Kevin Miller, "An Interview with Speed Leas," *Leadership Magazine* 2007. Available at www.alban.org.

8 One reason that gangs have been successful in recruiting young people in many North American cities is that they provide what families and religious congregations used to provide—a sense of meaning, identity, and belonging. The colors worn by gang members and the distinctive writing (graffiti) that members adopt are essentially the visible artifacts of that culture.

9 (2004)

10 (2004)

11 See William Bridges, *Managing Transitions: Making the Most of Change* (Cambridge, MA: Da Capo, 2003).

Endnotes

12 This represents the classic paradox of a system's view of organizational leadership. Organizational members tend to assume that leaders have much more power to effect change than they actually do. At the same time, when leaders change their own behavior to model desired behavior, that has far more impact than telling others what to do.

13 (2004)

14 (1983)

15 (2002)

16 (1998)

17 (Duncan 1972)

18 (1997)

19 Appreciative inquiry is a process of addressing issues and working towards change that stresses identifying and building on the strengths of a group, rather than only dealing with the problems or concerns it may be facing.

20 (Hatch 1997)

21 See Speed Leas, *Moving Your Church Through Conflict* (Bethesda, MD: The Alban Institute, 1985).

22 An interest-based approach seeks to find win-win solutions that satisfy the underlying needs and interests of both parties, whereas a rights-based approach seeks to determine if a party's rights were violated and how that can be redressed. Either approach may be appropriate depending upon the nature of the conflict or complaint.

23 For more on the Circle Process, see Kay Pranis, *The Little Book of Circle Processes* (Intercourse, PA: Good Books, 2004).

Selected Readings

Collins, Jim (2001). *Good to Great: Why Some Companies Make the Leap and Others Don't.* New York: HarperBusiness.

DiMaggio, Paul J. and Walter W. Powell (1983). "The Iron Cage Revisited: Institutional Isomorphism and Collective Rationality in Organizational Fields," *American Sociological Review* 48: 147-160.

Duncan, S. (1972). "Some Signals and Rules for Taking Speaking Turns in Conversation," *Journal of Personality and Social Psychology* 23: 283-293.

Greiner, Larry E. (1972). "Evolution and Revolution as Organizations Grow," *Harvard Business Review* 50.

Hatch, Mary Jo (1997). *Organization Theory: Modern, Symbolic, and Postmodern Perspectives.* Oxford: Oxford University Press.

Kotter, John P. and Dan S. Cohen (2002). *The Heart of Change: Real-Life Stories of How People Change Their Organizations.* Boston: Harvard Business School Press.

Schein, Edgar H. (2004). *Organizational Culture and Leadership* (3rd Edition). San Francisco: John Wiley and Sons.

Schneider, D. M., and C. Goldwasser (1998). "Be a Model Leader of Change," *Management Review* 87: 41-45.

Trahant, B., W. W. Burke, and R. Koonce (1997). "12 Principles of Organizational Transformation," *Management Review* 86: 17-22.

Weber, Max ([1947]1964). *The Theory of Social and Economic Organization*. New York: The Free Press.

METHOD OF PAYMENT

❑ Check or Money Order
  *(payable to **Good Books** in U.S. funds)*

❑ Please charge my:

  ❑ MasterCard   ❑ Visa
  ❑ Discover   ❑ American Express

_____

exp. date _____
Signature _____

Name _____
Address _____
City _____
State _____
Zip _____
Phone _____
Email _____

SHIP TO: (if different)
Name _____
Address _____
City _____
State _____
Zip _____

Mail order to: **Good Books**
P.O. Box 419 • Intercourse, PA 17534-0419
Call toll-free: 800/762-7171
Fax toll-free: 888/768-3433
Prices subject to change.

Group Discounts for

The Little Book of Healthy Organizations
ORDER FORM

If you would like to order multiple copies of
The Little Book of Healthy Organizations by David
R. Brubaker and Ruth Hoover Zimmerman for groups
you know or are a part of, use this form. (Discounts
apply only for more than one copy.)

Photocopy this page as often as you like.

The following discounts apply:

1 copy	$4.95
2-5 copies	$4.45 each (a 10% discount)
6-10 copies	$4.20 each (a 15% discount)
11-20 copies	$3.96 each (a 20% discount)
21-99 copies	$3.45 each (a 30% discount)
100 or more	$2.97 each (a 40% discount)

Free Shipping for orders of 100 or more!

Prices subject to change.

Quantity   *Price*   *Total*

_____ copies of **Healthy Organizations**   @ _____ _____

Shipping & Handling

(add 10%; $3.00 minimum) _____

PA residents add 6% sales tax _____

TOTAL _____